Bob's Odd Gifts

Written by Leya Roberts

Illustrated by George Ulrich

A Division of Harcourt Brace & Company

It is Farmer Bob's birthday.
The animals have big plans for him.

Digger Dog digs up some big bones.
"Farmer Bob will like this gift," he pants.
He puts them in a bag.

Tabby Cat catches six fat fish at the pond.
"Farmer Bob will like this gift," she purrs.
She puts the fish in a blue box.

Wiggly Pig finds some corncobs.
"Farmer Bob will like this gift," she oinks.
She wraps the cobs in pink paper.

Tad Frog catches some flies.
"Farmer Bob will like this gift," he croaks.
He puts them in a jar and closes the lid.

The animals dash into the barn.
They put on birthday hats.
Then they sit in the loft and wait.
At last Farmer Bob comes.

"Surprise!" yell the animals.
They all dance and clap for Farmer Bob.
He thanks Digger, Tabby, Wiggly, and Tad.
Then Farmer Bob looks at his gifts.

Farmer Bob opens his gift from Digger Dog.
The bones drop out.
“Hmmm. This is an odd gift,” says Farmer Bob.
He rubs his chin.

Farmer Bob opens his gift from Tabby Cat.
The fish flop out.
"Hmmm. This is an odd gift," says Farmer Bob.
He holds his nose.

Farmer Bob opens his gift from Wiggly Pig.
The cobs pop out.
“Hmmm. This is an odd gift,” says Farmer Bob.
He nods his head.

Farmer Bob opens his gift from Tad Frog.
Some flies hop out.
"Hmmm. This is ***really*** an odd gift," he says.
He twists his hair.

Farmer Bob opens one more gift.
"This is a cake," says Farmer Bob.
"My granny made it for me.
Would you like some?"

The animals look at the cake.
“We don’t like cake,” they say.
Farmer Bob thinks for a bit.
Then he gives them a wink.

He gives the bones to Digger Dog.
He gives the fish to Tabby Cat.
He gives the cobs to Wiggly Pig.
He gives the flies to Tad Frog.

The animals have their gifts.
And Farmer Bob has his cake.
Happy birthday, Farmer Bob!